4 Beloved Tales

Cinderella
stories around the world

by Cari Meister

PICTURE WINDOW BOOKS
a capstone imprint

What Is a Fairy Tale?

Once upon a time, before the age of books, people gathered to tell stories. They told tales of fairies and magic, princes and witches. Ideas of love, jealousy, kindness, and luck filled the stories. Some provided lessons. Others just entertained. Most did both! These fairy tales passed from neighbor to neighbor, village to village, land to land. As the stories spun across seas and over mountains, details changed to fit each culture. A poisoned slipper became a poisoned ring. A king became a sultan. A wolf became a tiger.

Over time, fairy tales were collected and written down. Around the world today, people of all ages love to read or hear these timeless stories. For many years to come, fairy tales will continue to live happily ever after in our imaginations.

Cinderella

A French Fairy Tale *illustrated by Valentina Belloni*

Once upon a time, there was a beautiful girl who lived with her stepmother and two stepsisters. The stepmother and stepsisters had very cruel hearts and treated the girl poorly. They made her do all the work: scrubbing the dishes, mopping the floors, washing the clothes, and cleaning their bedrooms.

The stepsisters dressed in the finest gowns and slept in the finest beds. The poor girl was given only rags to wear. She slept on a straw bed. The stepsisters called the girl "Cinderella," because her clothes were often covered in cinders and ashes from the fireplace near her bed.

One day, an invitation for the Prince's Ball arrived. The stepsisters were delighted! They spent the next few weeks picking out gowns and deciding how to style their hair.

Cinderella wanted to go to the ball too. But the stepsisters laughed. "You?" they said. "Certainly not. There is too much work for you to do. You must clean the entire house and help us get ready."

When the day of the ball arrived and the stepsisters left, Cinderella cried. "I wish I could go!" she said.

As soon as Cinderella said this, her fairy godmother appeared. She touched Cinderella with her magic wand. The girl's rags turned into a gown of gold and silver. On her feet were glass slippers.

Next, the fairy godmother turned a pumpkin into a coach. She turned six lizards into coachmen, a rat into a driver, and six mice into horses. "But," she warned, "when the clock strikes midnight, the magic will be gone!"

Cinderella's beauty stunned everyone, especially the prince. She and the prince danced all night. When the clock struck 12, Cinderella ran from the palace, losing one slipper.

The prince was puzzled. Who was she? How could he find her? All he had was one glass slipper. The next day he issued a proclamation: *I shall marry the girl who fits the slipper.*

The prince's servant traveled from house to house. He tried the slipper on every girl. It did not fit any of them. At Cinderella's house, the stepsisters tried. When the slipper did not fit, Cinderella asked, "May I try?"

It fit perfectly!

Cinderella's godmother reappeared and touched Cinderella with her wand. The rags were once again changed into fine cloth. And two days later, Cinderella and the prince married and lived happily ever after.

Little Burnt Face

illustrated by Carolina Farías

A Fairy Tale from the Micmac Tribe of North America

Once upon a time there lived a widower and his three daughters. They lived in a large village by the side of a lake. The oldest daughter was mean. The middle daughter thought only of herself. But the youngest daughter was kind and good.

Every day, when their father went off to hunt, the oldest daughter burned the youngest daughter with hot coals. She did this so often that the youngest daughter was covered with scars. The villagers called her "Little Burnt Face." When the father asked why his youngest daughter was always burnt, the oldest daughter lied. "I forbid her to go near the fire, Father," the girl said. "But she disobeys and always falls in."

On the farthest side of the village, in a beautiful wigwam, lived a great chief and his sister. The great chief was invisible. No one but his sister had ever seen him.

One day the chief's sister announced that her brother would marry any girl who could see him. Girls rushed to the wigwam.

"Can you see him?" the chief's sister asked. Many of the girls lied and said yes. Then the sister asked, "What is his shoulder-strap made from?"

The girls guessed. "A strip of rawhide."

"With what does he pull his sled?"

The girls guessed again. "A green willow branch."

Then the chief's sister knew they had not really seen him.

The next day, the widower's two older daughters went to the chief's wigwam. Little Burnt Face wanted to go too, but she had nothing to wear but rags. So she ran into the woods and peeled bark from the birch trees. She made herself a dress, a cap, and leggings. She borrowed her father's moccasins for her feet.

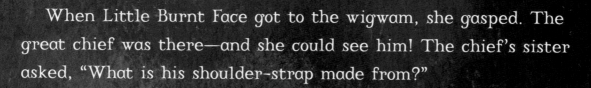

When Little Burnt Face got to the wigwam, she gasped. The great chief was there—and she could see him! The chief's sister asked, "What is his shoulder-strap made from?"

Little Burnt Face's sisters answered, "A strip of rawhide."

But Little Burnt Face said, "Oh no, it's the Milky Way!"

"And with what does he pull his sled?"

The older girls answered, "A green willow branch."

But Little Burnt Face said, "No. It's a rainbow!"

The chief's sister exclaimed, "You have truly seen him!" She bathed Little Burnt Face with dew, and the girl's scars vanished. The great chief also changed. He was no longer invisible.

Little Burnt Face and the great chief married. The whole village celebrated—except for the widower's two older daughters. They were driven from the village forever.

Yeh-Shen
A Chinese Fairy Tale
illustrated by Eva Montanari

Thousands of years ago in China, there lived a cave chieftain named Wu. He had two wives. His first wife was beautiful and kind. She gave birth to a daughter, Yeh-Shen, who was very much like her. Sadly, Yeh-Shen's mother died. Shortly thereafter, Wu died too.

Wu's second wife had a daughter named Jun-Li. Jun-Li and her mother were cruel and lazy. Without any other family, Yeh-Shen was brought into their home. They ordered Yeh-Shen to do all the work—collecting wood, washing clothes, and scrubbing the floor.

Yeh-Shen's only comfort was a golden fish that lived in the lake near the cave. Every day, she shared what little food she had with the fish.

One day Yeh-Shen's stepmother found out about the fish. She was furious. She did not want Yeh-Shen to have any joy. She captured the fish, cooked it, and served it for dinner. When Yeh-Shen learned what had happened, she wept. The fish had been her only friend.

But the spirit of the fish spoke to her. "Do not worry," it said. "Whenever you need something, just ask my bones."

Soon the New Year festival arrived—a time for singing and dancing, but also a time for men to seek wives. Yeh-Shen wanted to go. But her stepmother made her stay home. She didn't want Yeh-Shen to ruin Jun-Li's chances of finding a husband.

Yeh-Shen cried to the fish bones. As promised, the spirit fish took care of Yeh-Shen. It dressed her in a beautiful silk gown and golden slippers woven into a pattern of fish scales.

But the spirit fish
warned, "Be careful with
the slippers. If you lose
one, you shall hear from
me no more."

At the festival, everyone wondered who the dazzling girl was.

"She looks like Yeh-Shen," said Jun-Li.

Yeh-Shen panicked and ran, losing one of her slippers. A villager found it the next day. He sold it to a merchant, who then brought it to the king. The king marveled at the tiny slipper. He decided that the slipper's owner should be his wife.

Every woman in the land tried on the slipper, including Yeh-Shen. When Yeh-Shen put it on, it fit perfectly! Her rags turned to silk. She married the king and lived happily ever after.

Fate was not as kind to Yeh-Shen's stepmother and stepsister. It was said they were crushed by a shower of flying stones.

RHODOPIS

illustrated by Polona Kosec

AN EGYPTIAN FAIRY TALE

Long ago, pirates kidnapped a beautiful girl from Greece. They sold her as a slave to an old master in Egypt.

The master had several servants already working in his house. They made the new girl do the hardest work—washing the clothes, making the meals, and weeding the garden. They called her "Rhodopis," which means "rosy cheeked." Her skin was fair and turned red when she worked in the sun.

Because the servants were mean, Rhodopis made friends with the Nile River animals. After her work was done, she often went to the river's edge. There she talked to the hippopotamus and danced with the ibis.

One hot day the master spotted Rhodopis dancing by the river. "Someone with such grace should not go shoeless," he said.

He had a pair of rose-red slippers made for her. The other girls were jealous of the new slippers and treated Rhodopis even worse.

Not long after this, a message arrived. The pharaoh invited everyone to his court for music, dancing, and a feast. Rhodopis wanted to go, but the other girls would not let her.

"Sorry," they said. "Someone has to stay behind and do the chores."

They put on their nicest dresses and left.

Rhodopis went to the river to do the washing. But she couldn't stop thinking of the pharaoh's court. She forgot to take off her slippers, and soon they were soaking wet. Rhodopis put them in the sun to dry. *A falcon swooped down and snatched one of her slippers. Rhodopis was awestruck. She knew that the falcon was really the god Horus.*

Horus carried the slipper
over the Nile and landed at the
pharaoh's court. He presented
the slipper to the pharaoh.

"This slipper is a sign from
Horus," he announced. "Whoever
fits this slipper, I shall marry."

29

The pharaoh searched high and low for the slipper's owner. Many girls tried, but all failed.

At last he came to the old master's house. The servant girls tried the slipper. It did not fit. Then the pharaoh saw Rhodopis.

"Will you try it on?" he asked.

Rhodopis put on the slipper. It fit! The following day she and the pharaoh were married. Together they ruled Egypt for many, many years.

Glossary

chieftain—the leader of a clan or tribe

cinder—a piece of wood or other material that has been burned up or that is still burning but no longer flaming

cruel—willing to cause pain or suffering

culture—a people's way of life, ideas, art, customs, and traditions

ibis—a tall, slender bird that lives in and near ponds and lakes

pharaoh—a king of ancient Egypt

proclamation—an official announcement

widower—a man whose wife has died and who has not remarried

wigwam—a hut made of poles covered with bark, leaves, or animal skins

Beyond the Fairy Tale ...

Look at the illustrations for *Yeh-Shen*. What details tell you that the story takes place in China?

Pick two of the stories and compare them. What details do they share? How are the stories different?

Pick one theme used in the retellings, such as "good overcomes evil" or "don't judge a book by its cover." Explain how it varies in each story.

Read More

E Mei

Climo, Shirley. *The Irish Cinderlad*. New York: HarperCollins Publishers, 1996.

Manna, Anthony L., and Soula Mitakidou. *The Orphan: A Cinderella Story from Greece*. New York: Schwartz & Wade, 2011.

San Souci, Robert D. *Cendrillon: A Caribbean Cinderella*. New York: Simon & Schuster Books for Young Readers, 1998.

About the Author

Cari Meister has written more than 100 books for young readers. Her best-selling TINY series (Penguin Young Readers) has been in print for more than 15 years and has received numerous awards. Cari lives in Evergreen, Colorado, and Minnetrista, Minnesota, with her husband, their four boys, two horses, and one dog. Visit her online at www.carimeister.com.

3 1499 00501 7857

Thanks to our advisers for their expertise and advice:

Maria Tatar, PhD, Chair, Program in Folklore & Mythology
John L. Loeb Professor of Germanic Languages & Literatures and Folklore & Mythology
Harvard University

Terry Flaherty, PhD, Professor of English
Minnesota State University, Mankato

Editor: Jill Kalz
Designer: Ashlee Suker
Art Director: Nathan Gassman
Production Specialist: Katy LaVigne
The illustrations in this book were created digitally.

Picture Window Books are published by Capstone,
1710 Roe Crest Drive, North Mankato, Minnesota 56003
www.capstonepub.com

Library of Congress Cataloging-in-Publication Data
Meister, Cari, author.
  Cinderella stories around the world : 4 beloved tales / by Cari Meister.
    pages cm. — (Nonfiction picture books. Multicultural fairy tales)
  Summary: Retells the classic French version of Cinderella, along with three similar tales: Rhodopis from Egypt, Yeh-Shen from China, and Little Burnt Face from the Micmac Indians of the Canadian Maritimes.
  Includes bibliographical references.
  ISBN 978-1-4795-5433-1 (library binding)
  ISBN 978-1-4795-5449-2 (paperback)
  ISBN 978-1-4795-5441-6 (paper over board)
  ISBN 978-1-4795-5457-7 (eBook PDF)
  1. Fairy tales. 2. Folklore—France. [1. Fairy tales. 2. Folkore.] I. Cinderella. English. II. Title.
  PZ8.M5183Ci 2014
  398.2—dc23   2014006636

Photo credit: Steve Henke Photography, 32
4/28/15
Printed in the United States of America in North Mankato, Minnesota
042014   008087CGF14

Look for all the books in the series:

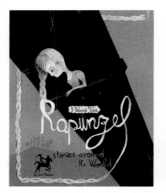

32